Easy and Delicious Fudge

Traditional and Specialty Fudge Recipes

Kathy E. Gary

First Printing, 2012

Printed in the United States of America

Disclaimer/Legal Notice
The information presented represents the view of the author as of the day of publication. Due to the rate at which conditions change, the author reserves the right to alter and update her opinions based on new conditions.

This book is for informational purposes only. While every attempt was made to accurately state the information provided here, neither the author nor her affiliates or publisher assume any responsibility for errors, inaccuracies or omissions. Any slights to people or organizations are unintentional.

Photo Credits
Thank you for sharing your amazing talent!
Cover Photo taken by Photophnatic

Easy and Delicious Fudge

Traditional and Specialty Fudge Recipes

Dedication

This book is dedicated to my grandchildren. I am so lucky to be your Grandma! I love you all to the moon and back and then some! Their love of everything sweet encouraged me to write this book.

Other Books by Kathy Gary

Passionate About Pierogies

Going Donuts For Paczki

Brunching on Bialys, Blini and Blintzes

Polish Desserts!

Kathy's Blog: http://kathygary.com

Table of Contents

Easy and Delicious Fudge

Introduction

Thank you for picking up *Easy and Delicious Fudge: Traditional and Specialty Fudge Recipes*!

As I write this, Thanksgiving is upon us and my granddaughter Anna, age 5, spent the past weekend with me. As always, much of our time was spent cooking and baking. Anna absolutely loves my peanut butter fudge and she asked me if I had included it any of my books. I told her that I had not, to which she commented, "That's too bad, Grandma. Everyone should taste this fudge." And with that, this book was born.

Many people shy away from making fudge because they 'just can't get it right' or they are afraid it will burn, or they just think it's too difficult. When I was younger and learning to make fudge, many times it ended up as ice cream topping instead, because it just wouldn't become firm. If you love ice cream like I do, that really isn't a bad problem to have. ☺ As with everything in life though, the more I made fudge, the easier it became and I have enjoyed experimenting to make a variety of specialty fudge which have been enjoyed by my family and friends over the years.

In this recipe book, I have laid out step-by-step directions, as well as detailed tips including links to videos to demonstrate temperature techniques. This should help eliminate guess work so that making fudge will be easy and foolproof for you as well. Truly by the second or third time you make fudge, it will be second nature for you.

My hope is that you will find the recipes in this book so easy that you will whip up a batch of fudge on a whim, whenever your crowd is clamoring for it, or whenever you need that moment of pure chocolate joy.

Happy Cooking!

~ Kathy

Tips To Make The Best Fudge Ever

Making fudge does not need to be difficult. If you know and follow these tips, you will be making fudge like a pro in no time!

Equipment: One important piece of equipment for making fudge is a **heavy pan**. I use a heavy two or three-quart saucepan. This size ensures that the pan is deep enough to minimize splatters.

You will also need a **good long-handled wooden spoon**. This type of utensil will not become hot during the fudge making process.

A **rubber spatula** can also be helpful. You don't want to scrap the saucepan as you empty the fudge into the pan. With a rubber spatula you can gently push out the fudge into the prepared 8-inch square pan.

One of the recipes below calls for a double boiler. I use this because this particular recipe is easy to burn, and with a double boiler you have more control over melting the chocolate slowly. A double boiler has a lower saucepan that contains water and an upper pan that contains the ingredients that you are melting/cooking. The ingredients melt as a result of boiling water in the pan underneath and helps to ensure that that the temperature is constant.

9

If you do not own a double boiler you can make your own by placing a mixing bowl (I suggest metal, glass or Pyrex) and a saucepan that the bowl will sit on top of. The two need to fit tightly together so that there is not a gap between the bowl and the pan. The bowl should also not be extremely oversized for the pan. To use the double boiler you simply fill the pan about half full with water and place it on low heat. Then place the ingredients you wish to melt into the bowl and place the bowl on top of the pan. Stir the ingredients frequently to ensure even melting.

Temperature Control
The most important factor in making fudge is being able to control the **temperature**. If you have failed in your fudge-making efforts in the past, it is possible that it is because the temperature of the mixture was not constant.

To ensure success, I suggest you use a **candy thermometer**. When using the thermometer, make sure the bulb does not rest on the bottom of the pan or the temperature reading will not be accurate. The accuracy of the candy thermometer is important. To test the accuracy of a candy thermometer, boil a pan of water and insert the thermometer. It should read 212 degrees F (100 degrees C).

If you do not have a candy thermometer you can determine the readiness of the fudge by dropping a smidge of the fudge into a glass of cold water.

When making candy there is the *soft ball stage* which is reached at a temperature of 232-240 degrees F, *the firm ball stage* which is reached at a temperature of 242-248 degrees F and the *hard ball stage* which is reached at a temperature of 250-268 degrees F.

To test for each stage, drop a bit of the fudge into a glass of cold water. When it has cooled remove it from the water. For the *soft ball stage*, the fudge ball should not disintegrate in the water and it should not flatten when you pick it up.

To determine if the fudge is in the *firm ball stage*, the fudge when dropped in cold water will form a firm ball that will not flatten when removed from water, but remains malleable and will flatten when squeezed.

To determine if the fudge is the *hard ball stage*, the fudge when dropped in cold water will form into a hard ball which holds its shape. The ball will be hard, but you can still change its shape by squashing it.

Rolling Boil. One other term you should be familiar with is the term 'rolling boil.' A rolling boil is when the substance is boiling rapidly.

If you would like to see what a rolling boil or soft, firm or hard ball texture looks like in candy making, you can search for these terms in youtube. There are a lot of great videos describing the candy-making process.

Tips Before Starting
Before starting, coat the inside of the saucepan with butter to keep sugar crystals from forming.

Line the pan that you will be placing the fudge in with aluminum foil allowing a few inches to fold over the sides. This way you can lift the fudge out after it has cooled. It makes cutting much easier than doing so inside the pan. Lightly grease the foil with butter.

Before beginning, have all your equipment and preparation ready. Once you start making fudge, you risk ruining the batch if you stop suddenly. So before you turn on the stove, butter the pans, measure the ingredients, and test the candy thermometer (see above for how to test a candy thermometer).

Tips While Making the Fudge

Once the fudge reaches 240 degrees F (115 degrees C) do not stir it or even shake the pan until it has cooled to about 110 degrees F (43 degrees C). After the fudge cools to 110 degrees F, beat the mixture vigorously with a wooden spoon. When the fudge stiffens slightly, it's time to add ingredients such as chopped nuts. Continue beating till the fudge becomes thick. At this point it will also begin to lose its gloss.

Tips After Making the Fudge

When pouring the fudge from the saucepan to the serving pan, don't scrape the sides or bottom of saucepan. Doing so could put sugar crystals into the fudge. I use a rubber spatula to 'push' the fudge out of the saucepan and into the prepared pan. If the fudge becomes too stiff, you can knead it with your hands until it softens. You can then press it into the pan. Spread the fudge evenly in the pan. While the fudge is still warm, it can help to score it into squares using a sharp knife. This will make cutting it easier when it has cooled completely.

Do not cut fudge until it has completely cooled.

Store fudge in the refrigerator in an air tight container. Fudge can be stored in the refrigerator for up to 2 weeks and in the freezer for about 3 months. It doesn't usually last that long in our home!

Traditional Fudge Recipes

Aunt Sarah's Chocolately Smooth Fudge

This recipe is one of my favorites, given to me by my Aunt Sarah. It is easy to make and difficult to goof up! It is also really enjoyed by everyone I have ever made it for. It calls for nuts, but if your crowd prefers plain, you can leave out the nuts.

Ingredients
1 1/2 cup granulated sugar
1 cup brown sugar
1 cup milk
2 tablespoons corn syrup
2 tablespoons butter
1/4 teaspoon salt
8 tablespoons dry cocoa
1 teaspoon vanilla extract
1 1/2 cup chopped walnuts

Directions
Line an 8 x 8 inch pan with aluminum foil. Lightly grease the foil with butter. Set aside.

Lightly grease the sides of pan with butter. (Doing so helps to prevent the sugar crystals from sticking to the pan resulting in grainy.)

In the pan over medium heat, combine all of the ingredients except the vanilla extract and the nuts. Stir until sugar is dissolved and mixture starts to boil. Carefully attach the candy thermometer to the side of the pan. Make sure that the bulb is under the liquid mixture but not touching the bottom of the pan.

Continue to cook the fudge until the temperature reaches 234 degrees F. If you do not have a candy thermometer, cook until the fudge reaches the soft ball stage. (See the Tips section for more information on the soft ball stage of candy making).

Remove your pan from the heat. Allow the fudge to cool until it reaches about 110° F.

With a wooden spoon, beat the fudge until it begins to stiffen. Add vanilla extract and nuts.

Pour the fudge into the prepared 8 x 8 inch pan. Do not scrape the sides of the pan. Instead, use a rubber spatula to push the fudge into the cake pan.

When the fudge has cooled, use the aluminum foil to lift it out of the pan.

Cut into squares and serve!

Melt-In-Your-Mouth Peanut Butter Fudge
For the peanut butter lover, there is nothing better than this fudge!

Ingredients
3 cups sugar
1 cup evaporated milk
1/8 teaspoon salt
1 pound creamy peanut butter
1/2 pound marshmallow fluff
1 tablespoon butter
2 teaspoon vanilla extract

Directions
Line an 8 x 8 inch pan with aluminum foil. Lightly grease the foil with butter. Set aside.

Lightly grease the sides of pan with butter. (Doing so helps to prevent the sugar crystals from sticking to the pan resulting in grainy.)

In the saucepan, combine sugar, milk and salt. Cook over medium heat until mixture begins to boil. Carefully attach the candy thermometer to the side of the pan. Make sure that the bulb is under the liquid mixture but not touching the bottom of the pan.

Continue to cook the fudge until the temperature reaches 234 degrees F. If you do not have a candy thermometer, cook until the fudge reaches the soft ball stage. (See the Tips section for more information on the soft ball stage of candy making).

Remove from heat and stir in the peanut butter, marshmallow fluff, butter and vanilla.

Continue to stir until ingredients are thoroughly combined.

Pour the fudge into the prepared 8 x 8 inch pan. Do not scrape the sides of the pan. Instead, use a rubber spatula to push the fudge into the cake pan.

When the fudge has cooled, use the aluminum foil to lift it out of the pan. Cut into 1 -2 inch squares.

Chocolate in My Peanut Butter Fudge

If you enjoy the combination of chocolate and peanut butter, you will love this fudge. The oatmeal adds a chewy texture.

Ingredients
1 cup semisweet chocolate chips
1/4 cup brown sugar
2 tablespoons soy milk
1/2 cup oatmeal
1/3 cup smooth peanut butter

Directions
Line an 8 x 8 inch pan with wax paper. Set aside.

This recipe is best made with a double boiler. (See Tips section above for information on how to make a double boiler if you do not own one).Place water in the bottom half of the double boiler and heat over medium. In the top half of the double boiler, combine chocolate, sugar and soy milk.

Turn heat down to low and continue to cook until the chocolate has melted. Stir in the oatmeal. Stir in the peanut butter by spoonfuls. Mix until it is spread throughout, but not thoroughly mixed in.

Line a small, shallow baking dish with wax paper. Scoop out the oatmeal mixture with a spatula and smooth it into the pan.

Refrigerate for 2 to 3 hours until it has firmly set. Lift the fudge out of the pan by holding onto the waxed paper. Cut into 1" squares.

Quick and Easy Vanilla Fudge

I use this recipe a lot when I need to bring a dessert to a pot-luck event on short notice. It is easy to make and I always have the ingredients in my pantry.

Ingredients
4 cup sugar
2 tablespoon butter
1 16 oz can evaporated milk
1 (8 oz) jar marshmallow fluff
1 teaspoon vanilla extract
1 cup chopped nuts

Directions
Line an 8 x 8 inch pan with aluminum foil. Lightly grease the foil with butter. Set aside.

Lightly grease the sides of pan with butter. (Doing so helps to prevent the sugar crystals from sticking to the pan resulting in grainy.)

In a heavy pan over medium heat, combine sugar, butter and evaporated milk, stirring constantly, until a temperature of 244 degrees F is reached. This is the firm ball stage when using the drop in water test. (See the Tips section for more information on the firm ball stage of candy making).

Remove from heat. Add marshmallow fluff and vanilla extract. Beat constantly with a wooden spoon until cool and creamy.

Pour the prepared 8-inch square pan. Refrigerate about one hour or until firm.

Sweet and Delicious Marshmallow Fudge

Ingredients
1 jar (7 oz.) marshmallow fluff
1 1/2 cups sugar
1 can (6 oz.) evaporated milk
1 1/2 sticks butter (3/4 cup butter)
3/4 teaspoons salt
12 oz. semisweet chocolate chips
1/2 cup chopped nuts
1 teaspoon vanilla extract

Directions
Line an 8-inch square pan with foil. Lightly butter the foil. Set aside.

In a heavy saucepan over medium heat, combine marshmallow fluff, sugar, milk, butter and salt.

Bring to a rolling boil, stirring constantly. Boil for 5 minutes more, stirring constantly.

Remove from heat. Add chocolate and stir until melted.

Stir in nuts and vanilla extract.

Pour into prepared 8-inch square pan.

Refrigerate about two hours or until firm.

Sweet Tooth Lovers Fudge

This fudge needs only a few ingredients, but is oh so fabulous! It is my young granddaughter's favorite!

Ingredients
2 pounds confectioner's sugar
2 cans (6 oz. each) evaporated milk
2 tablespoons butter
12 oz. semisweet chocolate chips
6 tablespoons marshmallow fluff
1 cup chopped nuts

Directions
Line an 8-inch square pan with foil. Lightly butter the foil. Set aside.

In a heavy saucepan over medium heat, combine sugar, milk and butter. Bring to a boil, stirring constantly. Boil 4 minutes longer.

Remove from heat and with a wooden spoon stir in the chocolate chips and marshmallow fluff.

Beat until chocolate melts and fudge thickens. Add chopped nuts.

Pour into prepared pan 8-inch square pan. Refrigerate for two hours or until firm.

Egg-ceptionally Good Fudge

This is the only recipe in this book that calls for egg whites. Fudge is not normally known to be 'light' but this recipe definitely results in a light and delicious fudge. For variety you can substitute 2 tablespoon grated orange zest for the vanilla extract.

Ingredients
2 egg whites
2 1/3 cups sugar
2/3 cup corn syrup
1/2 cup water
1/4 teaspoon salt
1/2 teaspoon vanilla extract

Directions
Line an 8-inch square pan with foil. Lightly butter the foil. Set aside.

In a large bowl, using a mixer beat egg whites to stiff peaks, set aside.

In a heavy saucepan over low heat, mix sugar, corn syrup, water and salt until sugar is dissolved.

Increase heat to medium. Cook, without stirring, to 265 degrees (or until a small amount dropped into cold water forms a hard ball. See the Tips section for more information on the hard ball stage of candy making).

As syrup cooks, wipe the crystals from sides of pan with a wet pastry brush.

Gradually pour hot syrup over egg whites in a thin stream, beating constantly at high speed until stiff peaks form when beater is raised.

Stir in vanilla extract.

Pour into prepared 8-inch pan. Refrigerate until firm.

Joy's Chocolate Syrup Fudge

My niece and I created this fudge one day years ago when we had a 'bake off' contest. It is still one of my favorites!

Ingredients
1 pound confectioner's sugar
1/2 cup nonfat dry milk
1 cup chocolate flavored syrup
1/4 cup margarine
1 teaspoon vanilla extract
1/2 cup chopped nuts

Directions
Line an 8-inch square pan with foil. Lightly butter the foil. Set aside.

In a large bowl, sift confectioner's sugar and non-fat dry milk together. Set aside.

In a small saucepan over medium heat, bring chocolate syrup to a boil. Remove from heat.

Stir in margarine.

Stir in sugar mixture about one-third at a time.

Continue stirring until fudge is thick and smooth. Stir in vanilla and nuts.

Pour into prepared pan. Refrigerate until firm. Sprinkle top with extra confectioner's sugar.

Quick and Easy Microwave Fudge Recipes

Rich Chocolate Microwave Fudge

Ingredients
2 cups miniature marshmallows
14 oz. can condensed milk
1 dash salt
12 oz. semi-sweet chocolate chips
1 cup milk chocolate chips
1/2 cup nuts
1 1/2 teaspoon vanilla extract

Directions
Line and 8-inch square pan with wax paper. Set aside.

In 2 qt. glass dish, combine marshmallows, milk, and salt. Place in the microwave on High for 3 1/2 minutes.

Remove from microwave and stir until marshmallows melt and mixture is smooth.

Add chocolate chips to the marshmallow mixture and stir until melted.

Stir in nuts and vanilla extract.

Spread fudge evenly in prepared 8-inch square pan.

Place in the refrigerator for 2 hours or until firm.

Turn on to cutting board, peel off paper and cut into 1 to 2-inch squares.

Just Plain Simple Microwave Fudge

Ingredients
3 2/3 cups confectioner's sugar
1/2 cup cocoa
1/4 cup milk
1/2 cup butter
1 teaspoon vanilla extract
1/2 cup chopped nuts

Directions
Line and 8-inch square pan with wax paper. Set aside.

In a 4-quart microwave-safe bowl, mix confectioner's sugar, cocoa, milk and butter.

Place in microwave and cook on High for 2 1/2 minutes. Remove from microwave and stir well.

Stir in vanilla extract and nuts.

Pour into prepared 8-inch square pan.

Place in the refrigerator for 2 hours or until firm.

Turn on to cutting board, peel off paper and cut into 1 to 2-inch squares.

Quick! 3-Ingredient Peanut Butter Fudge
Easiest fudge ever!

Ingredients
12 oz. semi-sweet chocolate chips
12 oz. peanut butter
1 (14 oz.) can sweetened condensed milk

Directions
Line and 8-inch square pan with wax paper. Set aside.

In a 2 quart microwave-safe bowl, melt chocolate and peanut butter on high power for 3 minutes. Remove from the microwave and stir well.

Add milk and stir until well blended.
Pour mixture into prepared 8x8 inch pan dish. Refrigerate until firm, about 1 hour.

Turn on to cutting board, peel off paper and cut into 1 to 2-inch squares.

Just a Taste of Chocolate Topped Fudge

Ingredients
1 1/2 cups sugar
1 can (5 oz.) evaporated milk
1/4 cup butter
1 jar (7 oz.) marshmallow fluff
1 cup chunky peanut butter
1 teaspoon vanilla extract
2 oz. semisweet chocolate

Directions
Line an 8-inch square pan with wax paper. Set aside.

In a 4 quart microwave-safe dish, combine sugar, milk and butter.

Microwave on high for 3 minutes. Remove from microwave and stir. Place back in the microwave and microwave for another 3 minutes. Remove from microwave and stir.

Place back in microwave and cook on high 4 to 6 minutes longer, until mixture reaches 238 degrees, or the soft ball stage. (See the Tips section for more information on the soft ball stage of candy making).

 NOTE: Do not place thermometer in microwave, place thermometer in liquid to check the temperate once the bowl has been removed from the microwave.

Add the marshmallow fluff, peanut butter and vanilla, beat until well blended.

Pour mixture into prepared pan 8-inch pan. Refrigerate until firm, about 2 hours.

Turn on to cutting board and peel off paper.

In a small glass measuring cup, place the semisweet chocolate and microwave on high 1 minute or until just melted. Drizzle the melted chocolate over the fudge. Cut into 1-2 inch squares.

Specialty Fudge Recipes

Krowki (Polish Fudge)

My mother would make Krowki for special occasions and it was such a treat for us! This recipe takes longer to make than most fudge recipes, but it is very much worth it!

Ingredients

1 1/4 cups plus 1 teaspoon milk
4 cups sugar
1 can sweetened condensed milk
1 1/2 sticks (12 tablespoons) butter
6 tablespoons powdered milk

Directions

Line a cookie sheet (with sides) with aluminum foil and butter lightly. Set aside.

In a heavy saucepan over very low heat, cook the milk, sugar and condensed milk for about 45 minutes stirring often.

Remove from heat. Add the butter and powdered milk and mix well.

Carefully pour out onto the prepared cookie sheet. Cut into squares while still warm. It will harden as it cools.

Silky Butterscotch Fudge

Ingredients
1 (14 oz.) can of sweetened condensed milk
11 oz. of white chocolate chips
11 oz. of butterscotch chips
1 teaspoon of rum flavored extract
1 teaspoon of butter flavored extract

Directions
Line and 8-inch square pan with wax paper. Set aside.

In a medium saucepan over medium heat, mix condensed milk, butterscotch chips and white chocolate chips. Stir until the mixture has melted.

Remove from heat and with a wooden spoon stir in the rum and butter flavorings.

Pour into the prepared 8-inch pan.

Refrigerate for an hour or until firm.

Turn on to cutting board and peel off paper. Cut and serve.

Chocolate Peppermint Fudge

I love the combination of chocolate and peppermint and I could eat this batch of fudge in one sitting!

Ingredients

1 2/3 cups granulated sugar
2/3 cup (5 oz. can) evaporated milk
2 tablespoons butter
1/4 teaspoon salt
2 cups miniature marshmallows
1 1/2 cups semi-sweet chocolate chips
1/2 teaspoon vanilla extract
1/4 teaspoon peppermint extract
1/4 cup crushed, hard peppermint candy

Directions

Line and 8-inch square pan with aluminium foil. Lightly butter the foil. Set aside.

In a heavy medium-sized saucepan, over medium heat, mix sugar, evaporated milk, butter and salt. Bring to a rolling boil, stirring constantly. Continue to stir constantly for 4 minutes. Remove from heat.

Stir in marshmallows, chocolate chips, vanilla extract and peppermint extract.

With a wooden spoon, stir vigorously until the marshmallows are completely melted. Pour into prepared 8-inch pan. Allow to cool slightly and then top the fudge with the peppermint candy.

Refrigerate for 2 hours or until firm.

Lift from pan and remove foil. Cut into 1 to 2 inch pieces.

31

Coco-Chocolate Fudge

This is such an easy fudge to make! No worries about needing a candy thermometer, and yet oh, so delicious!

Ingredients
1 cup semi-sweet chocolate chips
3 1/2 cups confectioner's sugar
1/2 cup cocoa powder
2 tablespoons butter
1/2 cup regular canned coconut milk
1/2 teaspoon vanilla extract
1 cup unsweetened toasted flaked coconut

Directions
Line an 8-inch square pan with foil. Lightly butter the foil. Set aside.

In a large bowl, mix the chocolate chips, sugar and cocoa together. Set aside.

In a small saucepan over low heat, combine the butter and coconut milk. Continue to cook and stir until the butter has melted and the mixture just begins to bubble. Remove from the stove and pour over the chocolate and sugar mixture.

With a wooden spoon, stir vigorously to mix all ingredients and to melt the chocolate. Continue to stir until mixture is smooth.

Mix in the vanilla extract.

Pour mixture into the prepared 8-inch square pan.

Sprinkle coconut flakes on top of fudge. Press gently on the coconut with your hand.

Allow to cool, or refrigerate, before cutting into squares.

Chocolate Krisp Fudge

When my daughter was young she would put Rice Krispies into everything, including milkshakes! So it did not surprise me when she requested 'rice krispy fudge' one day. This is the recipe we created.

Ingredients

1/2 stick (4 tablespoons) butter
6 oz. semisweet chocolate chips
1/4 cup corn syrup
1 teaspoon vanilla extract
1 1/2 cups sifted confectioner's sugar
2 cups Rice Krispies cereal

Directions

Line an 8-inch square pan with foil. Lightly butter the foil.

In a large saucepan over low heat, mix margarine, chocolate, corn syrup and vanilla extract.

Continue to cook over low heat, stirring constantly, until smooth.

Remove from heat and stir in sugar. Add Rice Krispies cereal. Stir until coated.

Press mixture in prepared pan (I use a lightly buttered spatula to make this easy).

Refrigerate until firm, about one hour.

Nutty Chocolate Mint Fudge

This recipe combines two of my favorite flavors: mint and chocolate. It is hard to eat just one piece!

Ingredients

1 (7 oz.) jar marshmallow fluff
1 1/2 cups sugar
2/3 cup evaporated milk
1/4 cup butter
1/4 teaspoon salt
1 1/2 cup mint chocolate chips
1/2 cup chopped walnuts
1 teaspoon vanilla extract

Directions

Line an 8-inch square pan with foil. Lightly butter the foil.

In heavy saucepan over medium heat, mix marshmallow fluff, sugar, evaporated milk, butter and salt.

Bring to a full rolling boil, stirring constantly.

Remove from heat. Add mint chocolate chips and stir until the chocolate chips are melted and mixture is smooth.

Add nuts and vanilla extract.

Pour into prepared 8-inch square pan. Chill until firm, about 2 hours.

Cut into 1-inch squares.

Time for the Holidays Fudge

This fudge is smooth and elegant tasting. It is so delicious with a cup of tea! I make it whenever I can find eggnog!

Ingredients

2 cups sugar
1 cup eggnog
1 tablespoon light corn syrup
2 tablespoons butter
1 teaspoon vanilla extract
1/2 cup chopped walnuts
2 tablespoons semisweet chocolate chips

Directions

Line an 8-inch pan with foil. Lightly butter the foil.

Lightly grease the sides of heavy saucepan with butter. (Doing so helps to prevent the sugar crystals from sticking to the pan resulting in grainy.)

In the saucepan over medium heat, add the sugar, eggnog and corn syrup. Continue to cook, stirring constantly until sugar dissolves and mixture comes to a boil.

Reduce the heat to medium-low and boil until mixture reaches 238 degrees F, or the soft ball stage. (See the Tips section for more information on the soft ball stage of candy making).

Remove from heat and cool to warm. Add 2 tablespoons of butter and the vanilla extract.

With a wooden spoon, beat vigorously until fudge becomes very thick.

35

Stir in nuts. Spread in the prepared 8-inch pan. Refrigerate until firm, about 2 hours.

In a glass measuring cup, combine chocolate and 1 teaspoon butter. Microwave on high 30 seconds or just until melted.

Turn fudge out on a cutting surface. Drizzle over top of fudge.

Cut into 1 to 2-inch squares.

Fudge With Liqueur

Coffee Liqueur Fudge
For the coffee lover, this fudge is just decadent!

Ingredients
3 cups miniature marshmallows
2 cups semi-sweet chocolate chips
2 ounces unsweetened chocolate baking bars, chopped
2/3 cup evaporated milk
1 1/3 cups granulated sugar
1/4 cup butter
1 cup chopped nuts (I prefer pecans).
1/4 cup coffee liqueur

Directions
Line an 8-inch square pan with foil. Lightly butter the foil.

In large glass bowl, combine marshmallows, chocolate chips and unsweetened chocolate. Set aside.

In heavy 2-quart saucepan over medium heat, combine evaporated milk, sugar and butter.

Bring mixture to a boil, stirring constantly; continue to boil for 6 minutes, stirring constantly.

Pour over marshmallow mixture and stir until the

marshmallows and chocolate are completely melted and mixture is smooth.

Stir in nuts and liqueur.

Pour into prepared 8-inch pan. Refrigerate until firm, about 2 hours. Cut into 1 to 2-inch squares.

Kahlua Fudge

Ingredients
1 1/3 cup sugar
1 (7 oz.) jar marshmallow fluff
2/3 cup evaporated milk
1/4 cup butter
1/4 cup Kahlua liqueur
1/4 teaspoon salt
2 cups semi-sweet chocolate chips
1 cup milk chocolate chips
1 cup chopped pecans or walnuts
1 teaspoon vanilla extract

Directions
Line an 8" x 8" pan with foil. Lightly butter the foil.

In a 3 to 4 quart heavy saucepan, over medium heat, mix together sugar, marshmallow fluff, milk, butter, Kahlua, and salt. Bring to a rolling boil. Stir constantly as it continues to boil, about 5 minutes.

Remove from heat, and stir in chocolates chips until melted.

Add the nuts and vanilla extract and stir to mix.

Pour into prepared 8-inch square pan and refrigerate for about 2 hours or until firm.

Cut into squares to serve.

Irish Cream Fudge
This fabulous recipe makes a lot of fudge and is perfect for a party or to give away as gifts!

Ingredients
1 1/2 cups butter
6 cups sugar
2 (5 oz.) cans evaporated milk
3 dark chocolate 8 oz. candy bars, broken into chunks
1/3 cup Irish Cream liqueur
1 teaspoon vanilla extract
1 (13 oz. jar) marshmallow fluff

Directions

Line two 8" x 8" pans with foil. Lightly butter the foil.

In a heavy saucepan over medium heat, mix butter, sugar and milk. Bring to a full rolling boil on stirring constantly. Continue boiling and stirring 5 minutes.

Remove from heat. Stir in the candy bars pieces until melted.

Add remaining ingredients; mix well. Pour into prepared pans.

Refrigerate until firm, about 2 hours. Cut into 1 to 2-inch pieces.

Final Thoughts

Fudge is a wonderful treat any time of the year. Many people shy away from making fudge because they think it is too complicated and the chances of failure are too great. If this has been you, I hope that you put aside your concerns and try a batch or two from the recipes listed in this book. Once you do, I am certain that making fudge will become a regular occurrence in your home.

If you enjoy this cookbook, please sign up to my email list through my blog, www.kathygary.com to receive updates on future books, free recipes and other goodies!

Wishing you happy creating, cooking and eating!

~ Kathy

Printed in Great Britain
by Amazon.co.uk, Ltd.,
Marston Gate.